The Moon

Melvin and Gilda Berger

SCHOLASTIC INC.
New York Toronto London Auckland Sydney
Mexico City New Delhi Hong Kong Buenos Aires

Photographs: Cover: Photodisc Collection/Getty Images;
p. 1: Werner H. Muller/Peter Arnold, Inc.; p. 3: Dennis Di Cicco/Peter Arnold, Inc.;
p. 4: Science Photo Library/Photo Researchers, Inc.;
p. 5: John Sanford/Photo Researchers, Inc.;
p. 6: Astrofoto/van Ravenswaay/Peter Arnold, Inc.;
p. 7: Peter M. Rosario/The Image Bank/Getty Images; p. 8: Kim Heacox/Peter Arnold, Inc.;
p. 9: Joseph Drivas/The Image Bank/Getty Images; p. 10: Galen Rowell/Peter Arnold, Inc.;
p. 11: Werner H. Muller/Peter Arnold, Inc.; p. 12: Astrofoto/NASA/Peter Arnold, Inc.;
p. 13: NASA/Scholastic Photo Library;
p. 14: Richard Wahlstrom/The Image Bank/Getty Images;
p. 15: NASA/Scholastic Photo Library; p. 16: Astrofoto/David Miller/Peter Arnold, Inc.

Photo Research: Sarah Longacre

ISBN 0-439-57478-1

12 11 10 9 8   6 7 8 9/0
                                                                    08

Printed in the U.S.A.
First printing, January 2004

The moon is a ball of rock.

Fun Fact

From Earth, we always see the same side of the moon.

The moon goes around planet Earth.

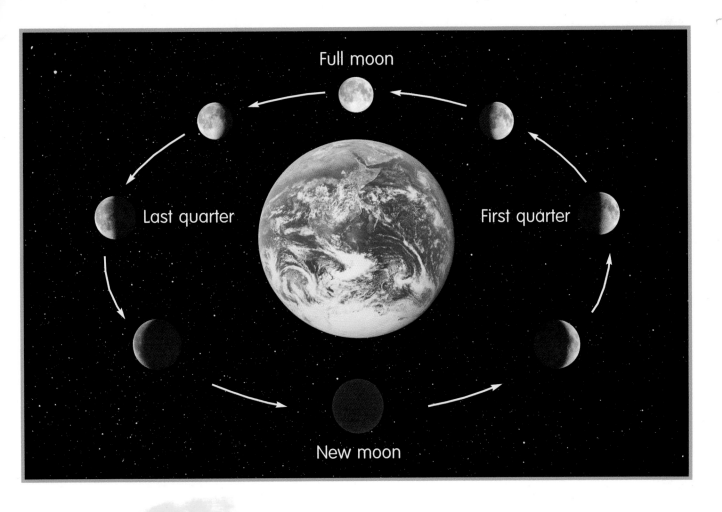

The moon takes about one month to go around Earth.

The moon is much
smaller than Earth.

Earth and the moon go
around the sun together.

The moon shines brightly.

Fun Fact

The moon does not make its own light.

The moon gets light from the sun.

Sometimes the sun lights one side of the moon.

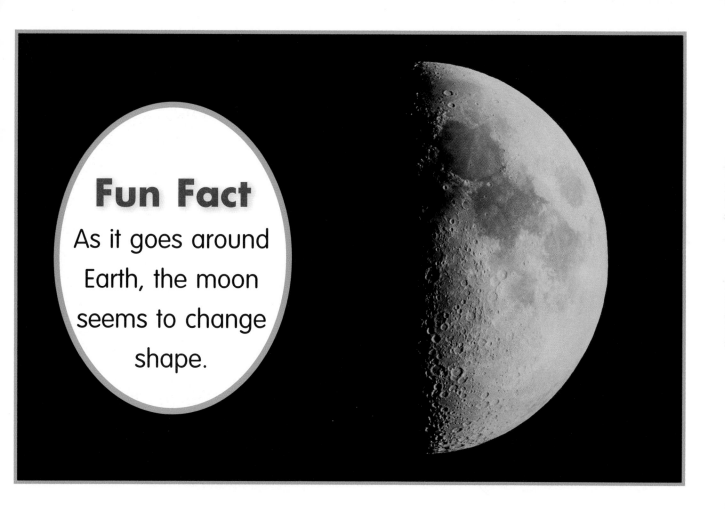

Fun Fact

As it goes around
Earth, the moon
seems to change
shape.

Sometimes the sun lights
only part of the moon.

Fun Fact

In the 1969 moon landing, Neil Armstrong wore a space suit to give him air.

The moon has no air.

The moon has no water.

Fun Fact

The holes were made by objects from space slamming into the moon.

The moon has many holes.

The moon has many
flat, dark places.

The moon is our closest neighbor in the solar system.